CW00968358

KINGFISHER
Larousse Kingfisher Chambers Inc.
95 Madison Avenue
New York, New York 10016

First American edition 1996
2 4 6 8 10 9 7 5 3 1
Copyright in this selection © Larousse plc 1996
Illustrations copyright © Lorna Hussey 1996

LIBRARY OF CONGRESS CATALOGING-IN-PUBLICATION DATA
The little book of cats / [selected by] Caroline Walsh :
[illustrated by] Larna Hussey. — 1st American ed.
p.   cm.
Includes index.
Summary: A collection of thirty poems celebrating cats and created
by a wide variety of poets.
1. Cats—Juvenile poetry. 2. Children's poetry. [1. Cats—
Poetry. 2. Poetry—Collections.] I. Walsh, Caroline.
II. Hussey, Lorna. ill.
PN6110.C3L57   1996
808.81'936—dc20   95-25191 CIP AC

ISBN 1-85697-679-3

Printed in Hong Kong

THE LITTLE BOOK OF

CATS

Selected by Caroline Walsh • *Illustrated by Lorna Hussey*

Kingfisher
NEW YORK

Contents

Cat Kisses

Sandpaper kisses
on a cheek or a chin
that is the way
for a day to begin!

Sandpaper kisses—
a cuddle, a purr
I have an alarm clock
that's covered with fur.

BOBBI KATZ

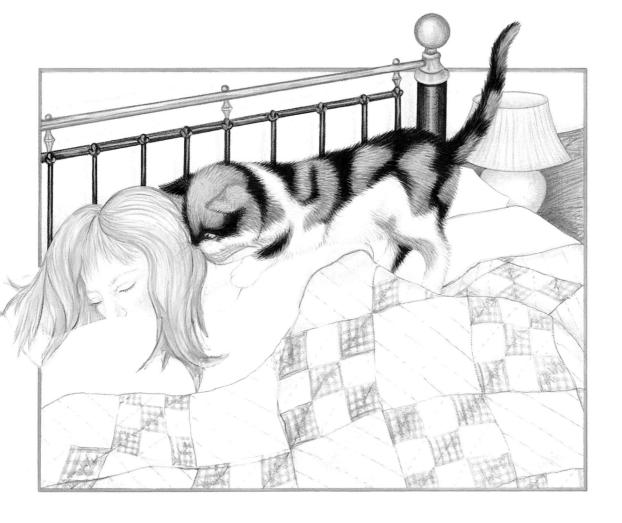

CATS

Are safe, and stealing sleep in quiet curls
around the house, keeping secrets to themselves,
easily. Their lips are sealed, their tails are question marks
or ride up behind them like dodgem car hooks.

We love cats. They shred the settee and we sit there
and let them, we buy them toys or collars with bells on,
we give them our names and the warmest places
and behind our backs they are licking their faces.

10

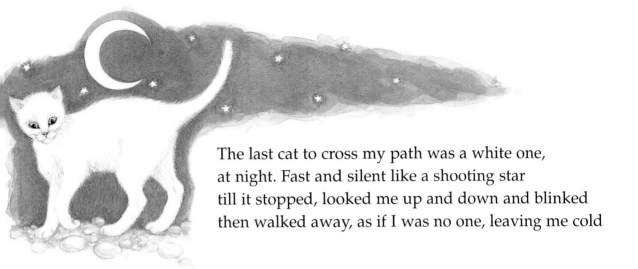

The last cat to cross my path was a white one,
at night. Fast and silent like a shooting star
till it stopped, looked me up and down and blinked
then walked away, as if I was no one, leaving me cold

as if I'd been caught, or photographed, or shot at,
or had my wallet stolen. Cats are something else,
worlds away, and we are welcome to it,
this lump of rock in space we call our planet.

SIMON ARMITAGE

11

Dame Trot and her cat
Sat down for to chat;
The Dame sat on this side,
And Puss sat on that.

"Puss," says the Dame,
"Can you catch a rat,
Or a mouse in the dark?"
"Purr," says the cat.

PUSSY

I like little pussy, her coat is so warm;
And if I don't hurt her, she'll do me no harm.
So I'll not pull her tail, nor drive her away,
But pussy and I very gently will play.

13

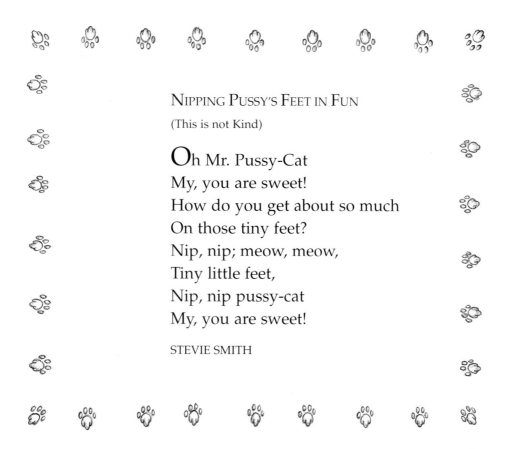

Nipping Pussy's Feet in Fun
(This is not Kind)

Oh Mr. Pussy-Cat
My, you are sweet!
How do you get about so much
On those tiny feet?
Nip, nip; meow, meow,
Tiny little feet,
Nip, nip pussy-cat
My, you are sweet!

STEVIE SMITH

POEM

As the cat
climbed over
the top of

the jamcloset
first the right
forefoot

carefully
then the hind
stepped down

into the pit of
the empty
flowerpot

WILLIAM CARLOS WILLIAMS

17

YOU

You are like the hungry cat
that wants to have fish
He won't wet his claws

MICHAEL ROSEN

(translated from Middle English)

IF YOU

If you,
Like me,
Were made of fur
And sun warmed you,
Like me,
You'd purr.

KARLA KUSKIN

GOOD HOMES FOR KITTENS

W ho'd like a Siamese?
Yes, please.

An Angora?
I'd adora.

A Tabby?
Ma'be.

A Black and White?
All right.

A Tortoiseshell?
Oh, very well.

A Manx?
No thanx!

COLIN WEST

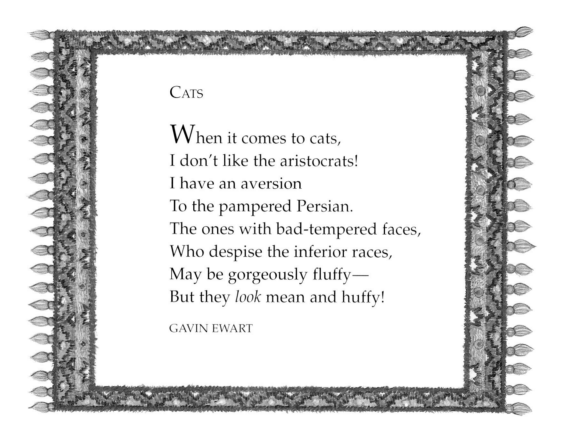

CATS

When it comes to cats,
I don't like the aristocrats!
I have an aversion
To the pampered Persian.
The ones with bad-tempered faces,
Who despise the inferior races,
May be gorgeously fluffy—
But they *look* mean and huffy!

GAVIN EWART

CAT

The black cat yawns,
Opens her jaws,
Stretches her legs,
And shows her claws.

Then she gets up
And stands on four
Long stiff legs
And yawns some more.

She shows her sharp teeth,
She stretches her lip,
Her slice of a tongue
Turns up at the tip.

Lifting herself
On her delicate toes,
She arches her back
As high as it goes.

She lets herself down
With particular care,
And pads away
With her tail in the air.

MARY BRITTON MILLER

DUET

My father once had a cat named Moose,
A big TOMCAT,
And he could whistle for him
Just like you whistle for a dog.
And my father would get a chair and sit down,
And when he came in, Moose would get in his lap.
Moose would whine, and my father would say:
Moose, where have you been,
I haven't seen you all day!
And they had the conversation on the front porch,
And nobody knew what they were talking about.

FRED RICHARDSON

LITERARY CAT

Dedicated to my great-aunt Marie

A fire, peace, and a book; all a cat wants.
The book's most important.

When humans don't watch and cats are warm,
Spectacles worn,
open slides the bookcase—
secret.
The Marvelous Adventures of Pussykins
is drawn from the shelf.
Happy now,
purring,
our hero puss not stirring,
purr, purr, purr.

RANJEET MOHAN GUPTARA

Where are you going,
My little kittens?

We are going to town
To get us some mittens.

What! Mittens for kittens!
Do kittens wear mittens?
Who ever saw little kittens with mittens?

Where are you going,
My little cat?

I am going to town,
To get me a hat.

What! A hat for a cat!
A cat get a hat!
Who ever saw a cat with a hat?

CAT PURRING

Cat
purring

four furry paws
walking

delicate-
ly
  between
flower stems
stalking

butter-
flies

KEITH BOSLEY

33

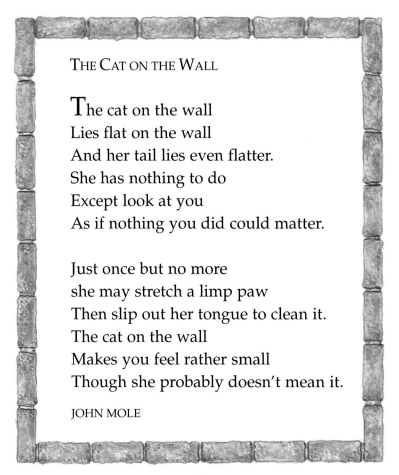

THE CAT ON THE WALL

The cat on the wall
Lies flat on the wall
And her tail lies even flatter.
She has nothing to do
Except look at you
As if nothing you did could matter.

Just once but no more
she may stretch a limp paw
Then slip out her tongue to clean it.
The cat on the wall
Makes you feel rather small
Though she probably doesn't mean it.

JOHN MOLE

from LADY FEEDING THE CATS

Shuffling along in her broken shoes from the slums
A blue-eyed lady showing the weather's stain,
Her long dress green and black like a pine in the rain,
Her bonnet much bedraggled, daily she comes
Uphill past the Moreton Bays and the smoky gums
With a sack of bones on her back and a song in her brain
To feed those outlaws prowling about the Domain,
Those furtive she-cats and those villainous toms.

Proudly they step to meet her, they march together
With an arching of backs and a waving of plumy tails
and smiles that swear they never would harm a feather.
They rub at her legs for the bounty that never fails,
    They think she is a princess out of a tower,
    And so she is, she is trembling with love and power.

DOUGLAS STEWART

CAT IN THE DARK

Look at that!
Look at that!

But when you look
there's no cat.

Without a purr
just a flash of fur
and gone
like a ghost.

The most you see
are two tiny
green traffic lights
staring at the night

JOHN AGARD

38

ALLEY CAT

A bit of jungle in the street
He goes on velvet toes,
And slinking through the shadows, stalks
Imaginary foes.

ESTHER VALCK GEORGES

THE CAT WHO COULD FLY

Every night he flies from the window-sill,
Over the hill,
Purring dizzily at the full moon,
Circling the land, valleys, rivers, and the sea;
Only thunder brings him down to earth
To an old lady's chamber.
In the daytime he sings sad songs,
And the world is silent,
For he cuts all tongues,
Sharper than a knife,
From meowing the nine secrets of his life.

The cat who could fly,
Never told a lie
And drank all tears
From the old lady's eyes.

FAUSTIN CHARLES

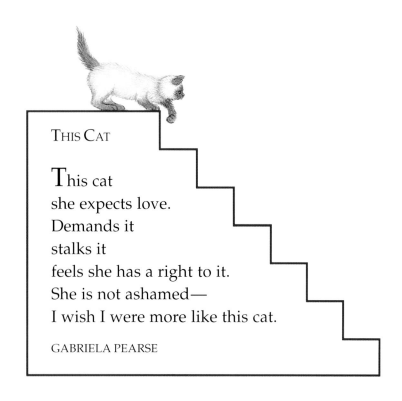

This Cat

This cat
she expects love.
Demands it
stalks it
feels she has a right to it.
She is not ashamed—
I wish I were more like this cat.

GABRIELA PEARSE

MOON

I have a white cat whose name is Moon;
He eats catfish from a wooden spoon,
And sleeps till five each afternoon.

Moon goes out when the moon is bright
And sycamore trees are spotted white
to sit and stare in the dead of night.

Beyond still water cries a loon,
Through mulberry leaves peer a wild baboon
And in Moon's eyes I see the moon.

WILLIAM JAY SMITH

from PANGUR BÁN

I and Pangur Bán, my cat,
'Tis a like task we are at;
Hunting mice is his delight,
Hunting words I sit all night.

When a mouse darts from its den,
O how glad is Pangur then!
O what gladness do I prove
When I solve the doubts I love!

Practice every day has made
Pangur perfect in his trade;
I get wisdom day and night
Turning darkness into light.

ANON

(Translated by Robin Flower)

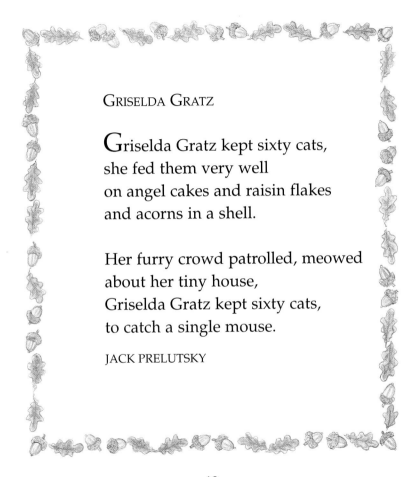

GRISELDA GRATZ

Griselda Gratz kept sixty cats,
she fed them very well
on angel cakes and raisin flakes
and acorns in a shell.

Her furry crowd patrolled, meowed
about her tiny house,
Griselda Gratz kept sixty cats,
to catch a single mouse.

JACK PRELUTSKY

CAT: CHRISTMAS

There's always
A ball or
A mouse,

Fondly
Packaged
And given,

Received
With gracious
Attention:

But the
Real success
Is the ribbon.

VALERIE WORTH

Diddlety, diddlety, dumpty,
The cat ran up the plum tree;
Half a crown
To fetch her down,
Diddlety, diddlety, dumpty.

THAT LITTLE BLACK CAT

Who's that ringing at our door-bell?
    "I'm a little black cat, and I'm not very well."
"Then rub your little nose with a little mutton-fat,
    And that's the best cure for a little pussy cat."

WANTED—A WITCH'S CAT

Wanted—a witch's cat.
Must have vigor and spite,
Be expert at hissing,
And good in a fight,
And have balance and poise
On a broomstick at night.

Wanted—a witch's cat.
Must have hypnotic eyes
To tantalize victims
And mesmerize spies,
And be an adept
At scanning the skies.

Wanted—a witch's cat,
With a sly, cunning smile,
A knowledge of spells
And a good deal of guile,
With a fairly hot temper
And plenty of bile.

Wanted—a witch's cat,
Who's not afraid to fly,
For a cat with strong nerves
The salary's high
Wanted—a witch's cat;
Only the best need apply.

SHELAGH McGEE

THE GREATER CATS

The greater cats with golden eyes
Stare out between the bars.
Deserts are there, and different skies,
And night with different stars.

VITA SACKVILLE-WEST

A catapillow
is a useful pet

To keep
upon your bed

Each night you simply
fluff him up

Then rest
your weary head.

ROGER McGOUGH

Index of Authors and First Lines

Acknowledgments

The publisher would like to thank the copyright holders for permission to reproduce the following copyright material:

John Agard: John Agard and Caroline Sheldon Literary Agency for "Cat in the Dark" from *Laughter is an Egg* by John Agard, Viking 1990 copyright © John Agard 1990. **Simon Armitage**: Simon Armitage for "Cats" copyright © Simon Armitage 1991. **Keith Bosley**: HarperCollins Publishers Australia for "Cat Purring" from *And I Dance* by Keith Bosley copyright © Keith Bosley. **Faustin Charles**: Walker Books Ltd. for "The Cat Who Could Fly" by Faustin Charles from *A Caribbean Dozen*, edited by John Agard and Grace Nichols, Walker Books Ltd. 1994. **Gavin Ewart**: Random House UK Ltd. for "Cats" from *Caterpillar Stew: A Feast of Animal Poems* by Gavin Ewart, Hutchinson's Children's Books 1990 copyright © Gavin Ewart 1990. **Robin Flower**: Oxford University Press for the extract from "Pangur Ban" from *The Irish Tradition* by Robin Flower, Oxford University Press 1947. **Bobbi Katz**: Bobbi Katz for "Cat Kisses" copyright © Bobbi Katz 1974. Used by permission of the author, who controls all rights. **Karla Kuskin**: HarperCollins Publishers Inc. for "If You Like Me" from *Any Me I Want to Be* by Karla Kuskin copyright © Karla Kuskin 1972. **Shelagh McGee**: Shelagh McGee for "Wanted—A Witch's Cat" copyright © Shelagh McGee 1980. **Roger McGough**: Peters, Fraser & Dunlop Group Ltd. for "A Catapillow" from *An Imaginary Menagerie* by Roger McGough, Viking Kestrel 1988 copyright © Roger McGough 1988. **John Mole**: Penguin Books Ltd. for "The Cat on the Wall" from *Catching the Spider* by John Mole, Blackie, Children's Books 1990 copyright © John Mole 1990. **Jack Prelutsky**: William Morrow & Co. Inc. for "Griselda Gratz" from *The New Kid on the Block* by Jack Prelutsky, William Morrow & Co. Inc. 1984 copyright © Jack Prelutsky 1984. **Vita Sackville-West**: Curtis Brown, London for "The Greater Cats" from *The Collected Poems of Vita Sackville-West*. **Stevie Smith**: New Directions Publishing Corporation for "Nipping Pussy's Feet in Fun" from *The Collected Poems of Stevie Smith* copyright © Stevie Smith 1972. **William Jay Smith**: Farrar, Straus & Giroux Inc. for "Moon" from *Laughing Time: Collected Nonsense* by William Jay Smith, Delacorte Press copyright © William Jay Smith 1990. **Douglas Stewart**: HarperCollins Publishers Australia for the extract from "Lady Feeding Cats" from *Selected Poems* by Douglas Stewart copyright © Douglas Stewart. **Colin West**: Colin West for "Good Homes for Kittens" from *What Would You Do With a Wobble-Dee-Woo?* by Colin West, Hutchinson's Childrens' Books 1988 copyright © Colin West 1988. **William Carlos Williams**: New Directions Publishing Corporation for "Poem" from *Collected Poems: 1909–1939, Volume 1* by William Carlos Williams copyright © New Directions Publishing Corporation 1938. **Valerie Worth**: The Estate of Valerie Worth Bahlke for "Cat Christmas" by Valerie Worth.